Geschichtenland: Englisch-Deutsch Geschichten für Kinder

Artici Kids

Published by Artici Kids, 2024.

While every precaution has been taken in the preparation of this book, the publisher assumes no responsibility for errors or omissions, or for damages resulting from the use of the information contained herein.

GESCHICHTENLAND: ENGLISCH-DEUTSCH GESCHICHTEN FÜR KINDER

First edition. July 2, 2024.

ISBN: 979-8224836123

Written by Artici Kids.

Table of Contents

Sparkle and the Missing Moonbeam - Sparkle und der verschwundene Mondstrahl

Once upon a glittering star in the magical land of Twinklewood, there lived a unicorn named Sparkle. Now, Sparkle wasn't just any unicorn. While other unicorns had soft pastel-colored coats and sparkly manes, Sparkle had a shimmering, iridescent coat that changed colors with every step. One moment she'd be a dazzling blue, the next a radiant pink, and then perhaps a golden yellow. But what made Sparkle truly unique was her horn. Instead of the usual pearly white, her horn was a prism of rainbows that glimmered in the sunlight and glowed softly at night.

Es war einmal in einem funkelnden Stern im magischen Land Twinklewood, wo ein Einhorn namens Sparkle lebte. Sparkle war kein gewöhnliches Einhorn. Während andere Einhörner weiche Pastellfarben und funkelnde Mähnen hatten, hatte Sparkle ein schimmerndes, irisierendes Fell, das bei jedem Schritt die Farbe wechselte. Einen Moment lang war sie ein atemberaubendes Blau, dann ein strahlendes Rosa und vielleicht dann ein goldenes Gelb. Aber was Sparkle wirklich einzigartig machte, war ihr Horn. Statt des üblichen Perlmuttweiß war ihr Horn ein Prisma aus Regenbögen, das im Sonnenlicht glitzerte und nachts sanft leuchtete.

One evening, as the sun dipped below the horizon and the stars began to twinkle, Sparkle noticed something peculiar. The moonbeam, which usually bathed Twinklewood in its silvery light, was missing. Sparkle's friend, Luna the owl, flitted down from her perch and landed gracefully on Sparkle's back.

"Sparkle, have you noticed the moonbeam is gone?" Luna asked, her big, round eyes wide with concern.

"Yes, Luna, I have. It's quite strange," Sparkle replied, her voice a melody of worry.

Eines Abends, als die Sonne unter den Horizont sank und die Sterne zu funkeln begannen, bemerkte Sparkle etwas Merkwürdiges. Der Mondstrahl, der Twinklewood normalerweise in sein silbernes Licht tauchte, war verschwunden. Sparkles Freundin Luna, die Eule, flatterte von ihrem Ast herab und landete anmutig auf Sparkles Rücken.

„Sparkle, hast du bemerkt, dass der Mondstrahl verschwunden ist?" fragte Luna mit ihren großen, runden Augen weit aufgerissen vor Sorge.

„Ja, Luna, das habe ich. Es ist ziemlich seltsam", antwortete Sparkle, ihre Stimme eine Melodie der Besorgnis.

Determined to solve the mystery, Sparkle set off on a quest, with Luna perched on her back. They journeyed through the Enchanted Forest, where the trees whispered secrets and the flowers sang lullabies. They crossed the Glimmering River, where the water sparkled like liquid diamonds, and ventured into the Crystal Caves, where the walls shimmered with a thousand colors.

In the deepest part of the Crystal Caves, they met a wise old tortoise named Shelly, whose shell was encrusted with precious gems.

Entschlossen, das Geheimnis zu lösen, machte sich Sparkle auf eine Suche, mit Luna auf ihrem Rücken. Sie reisten durch den Verzauberten Wald, wo die Bäume Geheimnisse flüsterten und die Blumen Schlaflieder sangen. Sie überquerten den Glitzernden Fluss, wo das Wasser wie flüssige Diamanten funkelte, und wagten sich in die Kristallhöhlen, wo die Wände mit tausend Farben schimmerten.

Im tiefsten Teil der Kristallhöhlen trafen sie eine weise alte Schildkröte namens Shelly, deren Panzer mit kostbaren Edelsteinen besetzt war.

"Shelly, the moonbeam is missing! Do you know where it could be?" Sparkle asked.

Shelly closed her eyes and thought for a moment. "The moonbeam is a magical thread that weaves through the fabric of

Twinklewood. If it's missing, it might have been stolen by the mischievous Shadow Sprites."

"Shadow Sprites?" Sparkle and Luna exclaimed in unison.

„Shelly, der Mondstrahl ist verschwunden! Weißt du, wo er sein könnte?" fragte Sparkle.

Shelly schloss die Augen und dachte einen Moment nach. „Der Mondstrahl ist ein magischer Faden, der durch das Gewebe von Twinklewood zieht. Wenn er fehlt, könnte er von den schelmischen Schattensprites gestohlen worden sein."

„Schattensprites?" riefen Sparkle und Luna gleichzeitig aus.

"Yes, Shadow Sprites," Shelly confirmed. "They love to play tricks and hide things. They live in the darkest parts of Twinklewood, where the light rarely reaches."

Determined to retrieve the moonbeam, Sparkle and Luna thanked Shelly and set off towards the Shadow Hollow, the darkest part of Twinklewood. As they approached, the air grew colder, and the shadows seemed to move of their own accord.

„Ja, Schattensprites," bestätigte Shelly. „Sie lieben es, Streiche zu spielen und Dinge zu verstecken. Sie leben in den dunkelsten Teilen von Twinklewood, wo das Licht selten hinkommt."

In the heart of Shadow Hollow, they found the Shadow Sprites, tiny creatures made of pure darkness with glowing eyes. They were playing a game of catch with the moonbeam, tossing it back and forth and giggling mischievously.

"Excuse me, Shadow Sprites," Sparkle called out, her voice echoing softly through the hollow. "The moonbeam belongs to Twinklewood. Can we have it back, please?"

The Shadow Sprites paused and looked at Sparkle with curiosity. "Why should we give it back? We're having so much fun!" one of them said.

Im Herzen des Schattenhohls fanden sie die Schattensprites, winzige Kreaturen aus reiner Dunkelheit mit leuchtenden Augen. Sie spielten ein Fangspiel mit dem Mondstrahl, warfen ihn hin und her und kicherten schelmisch.

„Entschuldigt, Schattensprites," rief Sparkle, ihre Stimme hallte sanft durch den Hohl. „Der Mondstrahl gehört zu Twinklewood. Können wir ihn bitte zurückhaben?"

Sparkle thought for a moment. "How about we make a deal? If I can show you something even more fun, will you give us the moonbeam?"

The Shadow Sprites huddled together, whispering and giggling. Finally, they turned back to Sparkle. "Alright, show us something more fun, and we'll give you the moonbeam."

Sparkle closed her eyes and concentrated. Her horn began to glow, casting a rainbow light that danced across the shadows. Slowly, the rainbow light began to take shape, forming into the most magnificent carousel the Shadow Sprites had ever seen. It was made entirely of light, with unicorns, dragons, and fairies as the carousel figures.

Sparkle schloss die Augen und konzentrierte sich. Ihr Horn begann zu leuchten und warf ein Regenbogenlicht, das über die Schatten tanzte. Langsam nahm das Regenbogenlicht Gestalt an und formte das prächtigste Karussell, das die Schattensprites je gesehen hatten. Es war vollständig aus Licht gemacht, mit Einhörnern, Drachen und Feen als Karussellfiguren.

The Shadow Sprites' eyes widened in amazement. "Wow! This is incredible!" they exclaimed, clapping their tiny hands in delight.

True to their word, they handed the moonbeam back to Sparkle. "Thank you, Sparkle. You've shown us something truly magical."

Sparkle and Luna took the moonbeam and made their way back to Twinklewood. As they returned, the moonbeam started to glow, casting its silvery light across the land once more.

Die Augen der Schattensprites weiteten sich vor Staunen. „Wow! Das ist unglaublich!" riefen sie aus und klatschten begeistert in ihre winzigen Hände.

Treue ihrem Wort übergaben sie den Mondstrahl an Sparkle. „Danke, Sparkle. Du hast uns etwas wirklich Magisches gezeigt."

Sparkle und Luna nahmen den Mondstrahl und machten sich auf den Weg zurück nach Twinklewood. Als sie zurückkehrten, begann der Mondstrahl zu leuchten und tauchte das Land wieder in sein silbernes Licht.

The residents of Twinklewood cheered and celebrated their return. Sparkle was hailed as a hero for her bravery and cleverness.

"Thank you, Sparkle," said the elder unicorn, Starbright. "You've saved Twinklewood from darkness."

Sparkle blushed, her coat shimmering with pride. "It was nothing, really. Just a bit of magic and a lot of determination."

From that day on, Sparkle was known as the unicorn with the most magical heart. And every night, as the moonbeam bathed Twinklewood in its silvery glow, Sparkle's coat would shimmer even brighter, a testament to her courage and kindness.

Die Bewohner von Twinklewood jubelten und feierten ihre Rückkehr. Sparkle wurde als Heldin für ihren Mut und ihre Klugheit gefeiert.

„Danke, Sparkle", sagte das ältere Einhorn Starbright. „Du hast Twinklewood vor der Dunkelheit gerettet."

Sparkle errötete, ihr Fell schimmerte vor Stolz. „Es war wirklich nichts. Nur ein bisschen Magie und eine Menge Entschlossenheit."

Von diesem Tag an war Sparkle als das Einhorn mit dem magischsten Herzen bekannt. Und jede Nacht, wenn der Mondstrahl Twinklewood in sein silbernes Licht tauchte, schimmerte Sparkles Fell noch heller, ein Zeugnis ihres Mutes und ihrer Freundlichkeit.

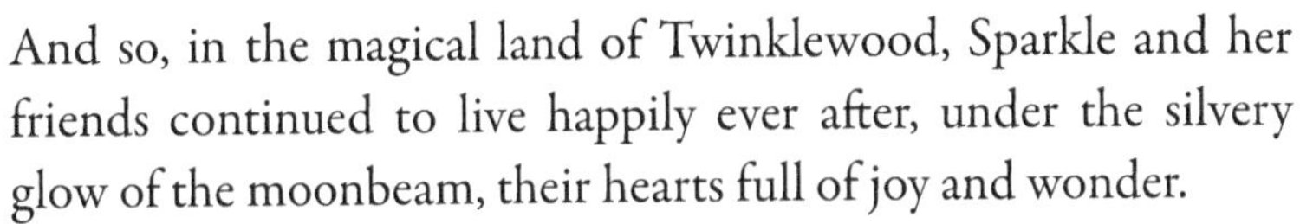

And so, in the magical land of Twinklewood, Sparkle and her friends continued to live happily ever after, under the silvery glow of the moonbeam, their hearts full of joy and wonder.

Und so lebten Sparkle und ihre Freunde im magischen Land Twinklewood glücklich bis ans Ende ihrer Tage, unter dem silbernen Schein des Mondstrahls, ihre Herzen voller Freude und Staunen.

Marina and the Great Underwater Mystery - Marina und das große Unterwassergeheimnis

Once upon a shimmering wave in the magical underwater city of Coral Cove, there lived a mermaid named Marina. Now, Marina wasn't just any mermaid. While other mermaids had tails of soft blues and greens, Marina's tail was a cascade of vibrant colors, shimmering in reds, purples, and golds. Her hair flowed like liquid silver, and her eyes sparkled like the clearest sapphires. But what made Marina truly unique was her ability to understand the language of all sea creatures.

Es war einmal auf einer schimmernden Welle in der magischen Unterwasserstadt Korallenbucht, wo eine Meerjungfrau namens Marina lebte. Marina war keine gewöhnliche Meerjungfrau. Während andere Meerjungfrauen Schwänze in sanften Blau- und Grüntönen hatten, war Marinas Schwanz ein Wasserfall aus leuchtenden Farben, schimmernd in Rot, Lila und Gold. Ihr Haar floss wie flüssiges Silber und ihre Augen funkelten wie die klarsten Saphire. Aber was Marina wirklich einzigartig machte, war ihre Fähigkeit, die Sprache aller Meeresbewohner zu verstehen.

One sunny morning, as the rays of the sun filtered down through the clear blue water, Marina noticed something strange. The

Great Coral Reef, which usually bustled with activity and was vibrant with color, seemed unusually quiet and dull. The fish that normally darted in and out of the coral seemed lethargic, and the corals themselves appeared pale and lifeless.

An einem sonnigen Morgen, als die Strahlen der Sonne durch das klare blaue Wasser fielen, bemerkte Marina etwas Seltsames. Das Große Korallenriff, das normalerweise vor Aktivität pulsierte und voller Farbe war, schien ungewöhnlich ruhig und trist. Die Fische, die normalerweise in und aus den Korallen huschten, wirkten träge, und die Korallen selbst erschienen blass und leblos.

Determined to uncover the mystery, Marina swam to the heart of Coral Cove, where the wise old turtle, Torto, resided. Torto's shell was covered in ancient carvings, and his eyes held the knowledge of centuries.

"Torto, the Great Coral Reef is dying! Do you know why?" Marina asked, her voice filled with concern.

Torto closed his eyes and thought deeply. "The Coral Reef is the heart of our city, and if it is sick, then something must be terribly wrong. I fear that the Pearl of Life, which gives energy and vitality to the reef, has been stolen."

Entschlossen, das Geheimnis zu lüften, schwamm Marina ins Herz der Korallenbucht, wo die weise alte Schildkröte Torto lebte. Tortos

Panzer war mit alten Schnitzereien bedeckt und seine Augen hielten das Wissen von Jahrhunderten.

„Torto, das Große Korallenriff stirbt! Weißt du, warum?" fragte Marina, ihre Stimme voller Besorgnis.

Torto schloss die Augen und dachte tief nach. „Das Korallenriff ist das Herz unserer Stadt, und wenn es krank ist, dann muss etwas schrecklich falsch sein. Ich fürchte, dass die Perle des Lebens, die dem Riff Energie und Vitalität verleiht, gestohlen wurde."

"Stolen? By whom?" Marina exclaimed, her eyes widening in shock.

"There are whispers of a sea witch named Morgana who dwells in the Dark Abyss. She has long coveted the Pearl of Life for its immense power," Torto explained.

Marina knew what she had to do. Gathering her courage, she set off towards the Dark Abyss, a place feared by all sea creatures. The water grew darker and colder as she approached, and the eerie silence was broken only by the occasional sound of distant, unseen creatures.

„Gestohlen? Von wem?" rief Marina aus, ihre Augen weiteten sich vor Schock.

„Es gibt Gerüchte über eine Meereshexe namens Morgana, die im Dunklen Abgrund lebt. Sie hat die Perle des Lebens schon lange wegen ihrer immensen Macht begehrt," erklärte Torto.

Marina wusste, was sie tun musste. Mutig machte sie sich auf den Weg zum Dunklen Abgrund, einem Ort, den alle Meeresbewohner fürchteten. Das Wasser wurde dunkler und kälter, je näher sie kam, und die unheimliche Stille wurde nur gelegentlich durch entfernte, unsichtbare Kreaturen unterbrochen.

At the edge of the Dark Abyss, Marina encountered a school of glowing jellyfish. Their gentle pulsating light provided some comfort in the oppressive darkness.

"Excuse me, glowing friends," Marina called out. "Do you know where I can find Morgana, the sea witch?"

The jellyfish floated closer, their lights flickering in response. "Beware, young mermaid," they said in unison, their voices echoing softly. "Morgana is dangerous and cunning. She lives in the deepest part of the Abyss, where the light cannot reach."

Am Rand des Dunklen Abgrunds traf Marina auf eine Schule leuchtender Quallen. Ihr sanft pulsierendes Licht spendete etwas Trost in der bedrückenden Dunkelheit.

„Entschuldigt, leuchtende Freunde," rief Marina. „Wisst ihr, wo ich Morgana, die Meereshexe, finden kann?"

Marina thanked the jellyfish and continued her journey. As she descended into the depths, she felt a growing sense of dread but pushed on, determined to save her home. Finally, she reached the bottom of the Abyss, where an eerie, greenish glow emanated from a dark cave.

Taking a deep breath, Marina swam into the cave. Inside, she found Morgana, the sea witch, holding the Pearl of Life. Morgana was surrounded by shadowy eels, their eyes glowing menacingly.

Marina dankte den Quallen und setzte ihre Reise fort. Während sie in die Tiefe hinabstieg, spürte sie ein wachsendes Gefühl der Angst, aber sie drängte weiter, entschlossen, ihr Zuhause zu retten. Schließlich erreichte sie den Grund des Abgrunds, wo ein unheimliches, grünliches Leuchten aus einer dunklen Höhle strömte.

Mit einem tiefen Atemzug schwamm Marina in die Höhle. Drinnen fand sie Morgana, die Meereshexe, die die Perle des Lebens hielt. Morgana war von schattenhaften Aalen umgeben, deren Augen bedrohlich glühten.

"Ah, Marina, the brave little mermaid," Morgana sneered. "What brings you to my humble abode?"

"Morgana, the Pearl of Life belongs to Coral Cove. You must return it!" Marina demanded, trying to keep her voice steady.

Morgana laughed, a sound that echoed ominously through the cave. "And why would I do that? This pearl gives me power beyond imagination."

Marina knew she needed to outwit Morgana. "How about a challenge? If I win, you return the Pearl. If you win, I will become your servant."

„Ah, Marina, die mutige kleine Meerjungfrau," höhnte Morgana. „Was bringt dich in meine bescheidene Behausung?"

„Morgana, die Perle des Lebens gehört zur Korallenbucht. Du musst sie zurückgeben!" forderte Marina und versuchte, ihre Stimme ruhig zu halten.

Morgana lachte, ein Geräusch, das unheilvoll durch die Höhle hallte. „Und warum sollte ich das tun? Diese Perle gibt mir Macht jenseits der Vorstellungskraft."

Marina wusste, dass sie Morgana überlisten musste. „Wie wäre es mit einer Herausforderung? Wenn ich gewinne, gibst du die Perle zurück. Wenn du gewinnst, werde ich dein Diener."

Morgana's eyes gleamed with interest. "Very well, little mermaid. What challenge do you propose?"

Marina thought quickly. "A singing contest. The one who can enchant the sea creatures with their voice wins."

Morgana smirked. "A singing contest? How quaint. Very well, let's begin."

Morgana began, her voice low and hypnotic. The shadowy eels swayed in time with her melody, their eyes glowing brighter. It was a dark and haunting tune, one that sent shivers down Marina's spine.

Morgana's Augen glitzerten interessiert. „Sehr gut, kleine Meerjungfrau. Welche Herausforderung schlägst du vor?"

Marina dachte schnell nach. „Ein Gesangswettbewerb. Wer die Meeresbewohner mit seiner Stimme verzaubern kann, gewinnt."

Morgana grinste. „Ein Gesangswettbewerb? Wie niedlich. Gut, dann lass uns beginnen."

Morgana begann, ihre Stimme tief und hypnotisch. Die schattenhaften Aale wiegten sich im Takt ihrer Melodie, ihre Augen leuchteten heller. Es war ein dunkles und unheimliches Lied, das Marina einen Schauer über den Rücken jagte.

When it was Marina's turn, she closed her eyes and sang a song of hope and light. Her voice was pure and clear, resonating through the cave and out into the Abyss. As she sang, the water around her seemed to sparkle, and the dull coral began to regain its color. Fish of all shapes and sizes gathered, their spirits lifted by her beautiful melody.

Als Marina an der Reihe war, schloss sie die Augen und sang ein Lied von Hoffnung und Licht. Ihre Stimme war rein und klar, hallte durch die Höhle und hinaus in den Abgrund. Während sie sang, schien das Wasser um sie herum zu glitzern und die trüben Korallen begannen, ihre Farbe zurückzugewinnen. Fische aller Formen und Größen versammelten sich, ihre Geister wurden von ihrer wunderschönen Melodie gehoben.

Morgana watched in disbelief as Marina's song enchanted the sea creatures. Realizing she had lost, Morgana let out a frustrated scream. "Fine, take your precious pearl. But know this, Marina, we will meet again."

With that, Morgana vanished into the shadows, leaving the Pearl of Life behind. Marina quickly grabbed the pearl and swam back to Coral Cove as fast as she could.

Morgana beobachtete ungläubig, wie Marinas Lied die Meeresbewohner verzauberte. Als sie erkannte, dass sie verloren hatte, stieß Morgana einen frustrierten Schrei aus. „Gut, nimm deine kostbare Perle. Aber wisse, Marina, wir werden uns wiedersehen.“

Damit verschwand Morgana in den Schatten und ließ die Perle des Lebens zurück. Marina schnappte sich schnell die Perle und schwamm so schnell sie konnte zurück zur Korallenbucht.

As Marina returned, the Pearl of Life began to glow, and the Great Coral Reef burst back into its vibrant, colorful life. The fish regained their energy, and the corals shimmered with brilliance once more.

The residents of Coral Cove cheered and celebrated Marina's return. She was hailed as a hero for her bravery and cleverness.

"Thank you, Marina," said the elder dolphin, Dolphino. "You've saved our home from darkness."

Marina blushed, her tail shimmering with pride. "It was nothing, really. Just a bit of courage and a lot of determination."

Als Marina zurückkehrte, begann die Perle des Lebens zu leuchten und das Große Korallenriff erstrahlte wieder in seinem lebendigen, farbenfrohen Leben. Die Fische gewannen ihre Energie zurück und die Korallen schimmerten wieder mit Brillanz.

Die Bewohner von Korallenbucht jubelten und feierten Marinas Rückkehr. Sie wurde als Heldin für ihren Mut und ihre Klugheit gefeiert.

„Danke, Marina," sagte der ältere Delfin, Delfino. „Du hast unser Zuhause vor der Dunkelheit gerettet."

Marina errötete, ihr Schwanz schimmerte vor Stolz. „Es war wirklich nichts. Nur ein bisschen Mut und eine Menge Entschlossenheit.“

From that day on, Marina was known as the mermaid with the most magical voice and the bravest heart. And every night, as the moonlight filtered down through the water, the Great Coral Reef would glow even brighter, a testament to Marina's courage and kindness.

And so, in the magical underwater city of Coral Cove, Marina and her friends continued to live happily ever after, under the shimmering glow of the Pearl of Life, their hearts full of joy and wonder.

Von diesem Tag an war Marina als die Meerjungfrau mit der magischsten Stimme und dem mutigsten Herzen bekannt. Und jede Nacht, wenn das Mondlicht durch das Wasser fiel, leuchtete das Große Korallenriff noch heller, ein Zeugnis für Marinas Mut und Freundlichkeit.

Und so lebten Marina und ihre Freunde in der magischen Unterwasserstadt Korallenbucht glücklich bis ans Ende ihrer Tage, unter dem schimmernden Schein der Perle des Lebens, ihre Herzen voller Freude und Staunen.

Freddie and the Flight of the Flamingos - Freddie und der Flug der Flamingos

Once upon a dazzling sunrise in the magical marshlands of Featherfield, there lived a flamingo named Freddie. Now, Freddie wasn't just any flamingo. While other flamingos boasted pink plumage from their diet of shrimp and algae, Freddie had feathers of brilliant blue. His beak was a striking gold, and his eyes sparkled with mischief and curiosity. Freddie's uniqueness made him both a marvel and a mystery among the other flamingos.

Es war einmal bei einem strahlenden Sonnenaufgang in den magischen Sumpfgebieten von Federfeld, wo ein Flamingo namens Freddie lebte. Freddie war kein gewöhnlicher Flamingo. Während andere Flamingos rosa Gefieder hatten, das sie durch ihre Ernährung mit Garnelen und Algen erhielten, hatte Freddie Federn in leuchtendem Blau. Sein Schnabel war ein auffälliges Gold und seine Augen funkelten vor Schalk und Neugier. Freddies Einzigartigkeit machte ihn sowohl zu einem Wunder als auch zu einem Rätsel unter den anderen Flamingos.

One breezy morning, as the sun cast golden hues across the water, Freddie noticed something unusual. The Great Feather

Tree, which stood tall in the center of Featherfield and was the heart of their community, had lost its magical glow. The tree's feathers, which normally shimmered in vibrant colors, were now dull and lifeless.

Freddie's best friend, Fiona, a flamingo with the fluffiest pink feathers, waddled over with a worried look. "Freddie, have you seen the Great Feather Tree? It looks sick!" Fiona exclaimed.

"Yes, Fiona, I have. This is very strange indeed," Freddie replied, his golden beak quivering with concern.

<hr>

An einem windigen Morgen, als die Sonne goldene Töne über das Wasser warf, bemerkte Freddie etwas Ungewöhnliches. Der Große Federbaum, der im Zentrum von Federfeld stand und das Herz ihrer Gemeinschaft war, hatte seinen magischen Glanz verloren. Die Federn des Baums, die normalerweise in lebhaften Farben schimmerten, waren jetzt matt und leblos.

Freddies beste Freundin Fiona, ein Flamingo mit den flauschigsten rosa Federn, watschelte mit einem besorgten Gesichtsausdruck herüber. „Freddie, hast du den Großen Federbaum gesehen? Er sieht krank aus!" rief Fiona.

„Ja, Fiona, das habe ich. Das ist wirklich sehr seltsam," antwortete Freddie, sein goldener Schnabel zitterte vor Sorge.

<hr>

Determined to solve the mystery, Freddie decided to seek advice from the wisest creature in Featherfield, an ancient heron named

Harold. Harold's feathers were as white as snow, and his eyes held the wisdom of many years.

"Harold, the Great Feather Tree is losing its magic! Do you know why?" Freddie asked as he approached the venerable heron perched on a tall rock.

Harold closed his eyes and thought deeply. "The Great Feather Tree is the source of all our energy and vibrancy. If it's losing its magic, it means the Feather Gem that powers it has been stolen."

Entschlossen, das Geheimnis zu lüften, beschloss Freddie, den weisesten Bewohner von Federfeld um Rat zu fragen, einen alten Reiher namens Harold. Harolds Federn waren so weiß wie Schnee und seine Augen hielten die Weisheit vieler Jahre.

„Harold, der Große Federbaum verliert seine Magie! Weißt du warum?" fragte Freddie, als er sich dem ehrwürdigen Reiher näherte, der auf einem hohen Felsen saß.

Harold schloss die Augen und dachte tief nach. „Der Große Federbaum ist die Quelle all unserer Energie und Lebendigkeit. Wenn er seine Magie verliert, bedeutet das, dass der Federstein, der ihn antreibt, gestohlen wurde."

"Stolen? By whom?" Freddie exclaimed, his blue feathers ruffling with alarm.

"There are whispers of a mischievous parrot named Percy, who lives in the Forbidden Forest. Percy has always envied the magic of the Great Feather Tree and might have taken the Feather Gem for himself," Harold explained.

Freddie knew what he had to do. With Fiona by his side, he set off towards the Forbidden Forest, a place known for its dense foliage and eerie silence. The further they went, the darker and thicker the forest became.

„Gestohlen? Von wem?" rief Freddie aus, seine blauen Federn stellten sich vor Schreck auf.

„Es gibt Gerüchte über einen schelmischen Papagei namens Percy, der im Verbotenen Wald lebt. Percy hat die Magie des Großen Federbaums immer beneidet und könnte den Federstein für sich genommen haben," erklärte Harold.

Freddie wusste, was er tun musste. Mit Fiona an seiner Seite machte er sich auf den Weg zum Verbotenen Wald, einem Ort, der für sein dichtes Laubwerk und seine unheimliche Stille bekannt war. Je weiter sie gingen, desto dunkler und dichter wurde der Wald.

At the edge of the Forbidden Forest, they encountered a wise old owl named Olive. Her eyes were large and round, glowing softly in the dim light.

"Excuse me, Olive," Freddie called out. "Do you know where we can find Percy the parrot?"

Olive hooted softly, her feathers ruffling. "Percy is indeed in the Forbidden Forest, but beware, for he is very tricky. He lives in the tallest tree, deep within the forest."

Freddie and Fiona thanked Olive and continued their journey. They moved cautiously, aware that Percy might be watching them from the shadows.

Am Rand des Verbotenen Waldes trafen sie eine weise alte Eule namens Olive. Ihre Augen waren groß und rund und leuchteten sanft im dämmrigen Licht.

„Entschuldigung, Olive," rief Freddie. „Weißt du, wo wir Percy den Papagei finden können?"

Olive gurrte leise, ihre Federn sträubten sich. „Percy ist tatsächlich im Verbotenen Wald, aber seid gewarnt, denn er ist sehr trickreich. Er lebt im höchsten Baum, tief im Wald."

Freddie und Fiona dankten Olive und setzten ihre Reise fort. Sie bewegten sich vorsichtig, da sie wussten, dass Percy sie aus den Schatten beobachten könnte.

Finally, they reached the tallest tree in the heart of the Forbidden Forest. High up in the branches, they spotted Percy's brightly colored feathers. Percy was busy admiring the Feather Gem, which glowed with an otherworldly light.

"Percy!" Freddie called out. "You must return the Feather Gem to the Great Feather Tree. Without it, our home is losing its magic."

Percy looked down, his eyes narrowing. "Why should I? This gem is so beautiful. It's mine now."

Freddie took a deep breath. "How about a challenge? If I win, you return the Feather Gem. If you win, you can keep it."

Schließlich erreichten sie den höchsten Baum im Herzen des Verbotenen Waldes. Hoch oben in den Zweigen entdeckten sie Percys farbenfrohe Federn. Percy war damit beschäftigt, den Federstein zu bewundern, der mit einem überirdischen Licht leuchtete.

„Percy!" rief Freddie. „Du musst den Federstein zum Großen Federbaum zurückbringen. Ohne ihn verliert unser Zuhause seine Magie."

Percy schaute nach unten, seine Augen verengten sich. „Warum sollte ich? Dieser Stein ist so schön. Er gehört jetzt mir."

Freddie holte tief Luft. „Wie wäre es mit einer Herausforderung? Wenn ich gewinne, gibst du den Federstein zurück. Wenn du gewinnst, kannst du ihn behalten."

Percy's interest was piqued. "Very well, what kind of challenge?"

Freddie thought quickly. "A flying race. Around the Forbidden Forest and back. The first one to return here wins."

Percy smirked, confident in his flying skills. "You're on, blue bird."

They took their positions, and Olive, who had followed them, hooted to signal the start. Freddie and Percy took off, wings beating furiously. The race was intense, with Percy leading at first due to his agility in the dense forest.

Percys Interesse war geweckt. „Sehr gut, welche Art von Herausforderung?"

Freddie dachte schnell nach. „Ein Flugrennen. Rund um den Verbotenen Wald und zurück. Der Erste, der hierher zurückkehrt, gewinnt."

Percy grinste, überzeugt von seinen Flugkünsten. „Abgemacht, blauer Vogel."

Sie nahmen ihre Positionen ein und Olive, die ihnen gefolgt war, gurrte, um den Start zu signalisieren. Freddie und Percy hoben ab, ihre Flügel schlugen heftig. Das Rennen war intensiv, wobei Percy zunächst führte, aufgrund seiner Wendigkeit im dichten Wald.

However, Freddie had a secret. His blue feathers weren't just beautiful; they were also aerodynamic, allowing him to glide effortlessly. As they neared the end of the race, Freddie pushed himself harder, flapping his wings with all his might. He caught up to Percy and, with a final burst of speed, crossed the finish line first.

Percy landed, panting and astonished. "You... you won. How did you do it?"

Freddie smiled. "Sometimes, being different gives you an advantage."

Percy sighed, but a smile tugged at his beak. "Fair is fair. Here, take the Feather Gem."

Doch Freddie hatte ein Geheimnis. Seine blauen Federn waren nicht nur schön, sondern auch aerodynamisch, sodass er mühelos gleiten konnte. Als sie sich dem Ende des Rennens näherten, strengte sich Freddie noch mehr an, schlug mit aller Kraft mit den Flügeln. Er holte Percy ein und überquerte mit einem letzten Geschwindigkeitsschub als Erster die Ziellinie.

Percy landete, keuchend und erstaunt. „Du... du hast gewonnen. Wie hast du das gemacht?"

Freddie lächelte. „Manchmal verschafft einem Anderssein einen Vorteil."

Percy seufzte, aber ein Lächeln zog an seinem Schnabel. „Fair ist fair. Hier, nimm den Federstein."

Freddie and Fiona thanked Percy and hurried back to Featherfield. As soon as they placed the Feather Gem back in the Great Feather Tree, the tree began to glow with a brilliant light. The feathers regained their vibrant colors, and the marshlands were once again filled with energy and life.

The residents of Featherfield cheered and celebrated Freddie's return. He was hailed as a hero for his bravery and cleverness.

"Thank you, Freddie," said the elder pelican, Pelly. "You've saved our home from darkness."

Freddie blushed, his blue feathers shimmering with pride. "It was nothing, really. Just a bit of teamwork and a lot of determination."

Freddie und Fiona dankten Percy und eilten zurück nach Federfeld. Sobald sie den Federstein zurück in den Großen Federbaum legten, begann der Baum mit einem strahlenden Licht zu leuchten. Die Federn gewannen ihre lebhaften Farben zurück und die Sumpfgebiete waren wieder voller Energie und Leben.

Die Bewohner von Federfeld jubelten und feierten Freddies Rückkehr. Er wurde als Held für seinen Mut und seine Klugheit gefeiert.

„Danke, Freddie," sagte der ältere Pelikan Pelly. „Du hast unser Zuhause vor der Dunkelheit gerettet."

Freddie errötete, seine blauen Federn schimmerten vor Stolz. „Es war wirklich nichts. Nur ein bisschen Teamarbeit und eine Menge Entschlossenheit."

From that day on, Freddie was known as the flamingo with the most magical feathers and the bravest heart. And every evening, as the sun set over Featherfield, the Great Feather Tree would glow even brighter, a testament to Freddie's courage and kindness.

And so, in the magical marshlands of Featherfield, Freddie and his friends continued to live happily ever after, under the shimmering glow of the Great Feather Tree, their hearts full of joy and wonder.

Von diesem Tag an war Freddie als der Flamingo mit den magischsten Federn und dem mutigsten Herzen bekannt. Und jeden Abend, wenn die Sonne über Federfeld unterging, leuchtete der Große Federbaum noch heller, ein Zeugnis für Freddies Mut und Freundlichkeit.

Und so lebten Freddie und seine Freunde in den magischen Sumpfgebieten von Federfeld glücklich bis ans Ende ihrer Tage, unter dem schimmernden Glanz des Großen Federbaums, ihre Herzen voller Freude und Staunen.

Duncan the Dazzling Donkey - Duncan, der bezaubernde Esel

Once upon a time, in the lush and rolling hills of Dapplewood, there lived a donkey named Duncan. But Duncan wasn't just any donkey. While most donkeys had dull gray coats, Duncan's coat shimmered with a rainbow of colors that changed depending on his mood. When he was happy, he gleamed with vibrant blues and purples; when he was sad, his coat turned a deep, solemn indigo.

Es war einmal, in den üppigen und hügeligen Landschaften von Dapplewood, lebte ein Esel namens Duncan. Aber Duncan war kein gewöhnlicher Esel. Während die meisten Esel ein stumpfes graues Fell hatten, schimmerte Duncans Fell in einem Regenbogen von Farben, die sich je nach seiner Stimmung änderten. Wenn er glücklich war, glänzte er in lebhaften Blau- und Violetttönen; wenn er traurig war, wurde sein Fell tief und feierlich indigoblau.

Despite his dazzling appearance, Duncan felt out of place. The other animals in Dapplewood, especially the plain gray donkeys, often teased him. They didn't understand his magical coat and thought it was silly.

"Look at Duncan, the rainbow donkey!" they would laugh. "You'll never blend in with us normal donkeys!"

One day, Duncan decided he had had enough. He would leave Dapplewood and find a place where he belonged. He packed a small bundle of his favorite snacks—carrots and apples—and set off on his journey, his coat glistening with determination.

Trotz seines bezaubernden Aussehens fühlte sich Duncan fehl am Platz. Die anderen Tiere in Dapplewood, besonders die schlichten grauen Esel, neckten ihn oft. Sie verstanden sein magisches Fell nicht und hielten es für albern.

„Schaut euch Duncan an, den Regenbogenesel!" lachten sie. „Du wirst dich niemals unter uns normale Esel mischen!"

Eines Tages beschloss Duncan, dass er genug hatte. Er würde Dapplewood verlassen und einen Ort finden, an dem er hingehörte. Er packte ein kleines Bündel seiner Lieblingssnacks – Karotten und Äpfel – und machte sich auf den Weg, sein Fell glitzerte vor Entschlossenheit.

As Duncan wandered through the vast meadows and dense forests, he came across many animals who were astonished by his colorful coat. There was a family of rabbits who gasped in awe, a wise old owl who hooted in surprise, and even a deer who mistook him for a walking rainbow.

After days of traveling, Duncan arrived at a quaint village at the edge of a sparkling lake. The village was unlike any place he had seen before. The houses were painted in bright, cheerful colors, and the streets were lined with flower gardens bursting with every hue imaginable.

Während Duncan durch die weiten Wiesen und dichten Wälder wanderte, traf er auf viele Tiere, die von seinem bunten Fell erstaunt waren. Da war eine Familie von Kaninchen, die vor Ehrfurcht keuchten, eine weise alte Eule, die überrascht hupte, und sogar ein Hirsch, der ihn für einen wandelnden Regenbogen hielt.

Nach Tagen des Reisens kam Duncan in einem malerischen Dorf am Rande eines funkelnden Sees an. Das Dorf war anders als jeder Ort, den er zuvor gesehen hatte. Die Häuser waren in leuchtenden, fröhlichen Farben gestrichen und die Straßen waren gesäumt von Blumengärten, die in allen erdenklichen Farben erblühten.

The villagers, humans and animals alike, welcomed Duncan with open arms. They had never seen such a magnificent creature and were fascinated by his changing coat. Duncan quickly became the star of the village. Children would run up to him, laughing and trying to guess what color his coat would turn next.

One day, the village elder, a kind-hearted woman named Eliza, invited Duncan to her cottage for tea. Eliza's cottage was a cozy little place filled with books and trinkets from her travels around the world.

Die Dorfbewohner, Menschen und Tiere gleichermaßen, empfingen Duncan mit offenen Armen. Sie hatten noch nie ein so prächtiges Wesen gesehen und waren fasziniert von seinem sich ändernden Fell. Duncan wurde schnell der Star des Dorfes. Kinder rannten zu ihm, lachten und versuchten zu erraten, welche Farbe sein Fell als nächstes annehmen würde.

Eines Tages lud die Dorfälteste, eine gutherzige Frau namens Eliza, Duncan zu sich in ihr Häuschen zum Tee ein. Elizas Häuschen war ein gemütlicher kleiner Ort, gefüllt mit Büchern und Andenken von ihren Reisen rund um die Welt.

"Duncan," Eliza began as she poured him a cup of chamomile tea, "I've heard many stories of magical creatures, but you are the first I've ever met. Your coat is truly special. Do you know why it changes color?"

Duncan shook his head. "I've always been like this. It's just how I am. But the other donkeys back in Dapplewood didn't like it. They said I would never fit in."

Eliza smiled warmly. "Being different is a gift, not a curse. Your colors bring joy and wonder to this village. Never let anyone make you feel like you don't belong. In fact, I think you were meant to bring magic to those who need it most."

„Duncan,“ begann Eliza, während sie ihm eine Tasse Kamillentee einschenkte, „ich habe viele Geschichten über magische Kreaturen gehört, aber du bist der erste, den ich je getroffen habe. Dein Fell ist wirklich etwas Besonderes. Weißt du, warum es die Farbe wechselt?“

Duncan schüttelte den Kopf. „Ich war schon immer so. Es ist einfach, wie ich bin. Aber die anderen Esel in Dapplewood mochten es nicht. Sie sagten, ich würde nie dazugehören.“

Eliza lächelte warm. „Anders zu sein ist ein Geschenk, kein Fluch. Deine Farben bringen Freude und Staunen in dieses Dorf. Lass niemals zu, dass jemand dich glauben lässt, du gehörst nicht dazu. Tatsächlich denke ich, dass du dazu bestimmt bist, Magie dorthin zu bringen, wo sie am meisten gebraucht wird.“

Duncan felt a warm glow inside, and his coat shimmered with brilliant gold. For the first time, he felt truly appreciated and understood. From that day on, Duncan made it his mission to spread joy wherever he went. He visited neighboring villages, performed at festivals, and even helped to lift the spirits of those who were sad or lonely.

One autumn afternoon, while Duncan was entertaining a group of children with his colorful tricks, a frantic squirrel named Squeaky approached him. "Duncan, you have to come quickly! The Great Oak in our forest is dying, and we don't know why!"

Duncan fühlte ein warmes Glühen in sich und sein Fell schimmerte in strahlendem Gold. Zum ersten Mal fühlte er sich wirklich geschätzt und verstanden. Von diesem Tag an machte es sich Duncan zur Aufgabe, überall Freude zu verbreiten, wohin er auch ging. Er besuchte benachbarte Dörfer, trat auf Festivals auf und half sogar, die Geister derer zu heben, die traurig oder einsam waren.

An einem Herbstnachmittag, als Duncan eine Gruppe von Kindern mit seinen bunten Tricks unterhielt, kam ein aufgeregtes Eichhörnchen namens Squeaky auf ihn zu. „Duncan, du musst schnell kommen! Die Große Eiche in unserem Wald stirbt und wir wissen nicht warum!"

Duncan didn't hesitate. He followed Squeaky through the forest to the Great Oak, the oldest and most revered tree in the land. When they arrived, Duncan saw that the tree's leaves were brown and withered, and its trunk was dull and lifeless.

"What happened?" Duncan asked the gathering animals.

"We don't know," said Squeaky, his voice trembling. "The Great Oak has always been strong and healthy. We think someone might have taken the Heartwood Gem from its roots. Without it, the tree cannot survive."

Duncan zögerte nicht. Er folgte Squeaky durch den Wald zur Großen Eiche, dem ältesten und am meisten verehrten Baum des Landes. Als sie ankamen, sah Duncan, dass die Blätter des Baumes braun und verwelkt waren und sein Stamm stumpf und leblos wirkte.

„Was ist passiert?" fragte Duncan die versammelten Tiere.

„Wir wissen es nicht," sagte Squeaky, seine Stimme zitterte. „Die Große Eiche war immer stark und gesund. Wir denken, jemand könnte das Kernholz-Juwel aus seinen Wurzeln genommen haben. Ohne es kann der Baum nicht überleben."

Determined to save the Great Oak, Duncan set out to find the Heartwood Gem. He searched high and low, asking every creature he met if they had seen it. After days of searching, Duncan found himself at the edge of a dark, foreboding cave. A grumpy old badger named Benny emerged from the shadows.

"What do you want?" Benny growled.

"Please, Benny," Duncan pleaded. "The Great Oak is dying. We think the Heartwood Gem was stolen. Have you seen it?"

Benny's eyes softened slightly. "I might have seen something like that. It was taken by a greedy raccoon named Rocky. He lives in a burrow on the other side of the forest."

Entschlossen, die Große Eiche zu retten, machte sich Duncan auf die Suche nach dem Kernholz-Juwel. Er suchte hoch und niedrig und fragte jedes Wesen, das er traf, ob es das Juwel gesehen hätte. Nach Tagen des Suchens fand sich Duncan am Rande einer dunklen, unheilvollen Höhle wieder. Ein mürrischer alter Dachs namens Benny tauchte aus den Schatten auf.

„Was willst du?" knurrte Benny.

„Bitte, Benny," flehte Duncan. „Die Große Eiche stirbt. Wir denken, dass das Kernholz-Juwel gestohlen wurde. Hast du es gesehen?"

Bennys Augen wurden etwas weicher. „Vielleicht habe ich so etwas gesehen. Es wurde von einem gierigen Waschbären namens Rocky genommen. Er lebt in einem Bau auf der anderen Seite des Waldes."

———

Duncan thanked Benny and hurried off to find Rocky. When he reached Rocky's burrow, he saw the raccoon admiring the Heartwood Gem, its green glow lighting up the den.

"Rocky, you must return the Heartwood Gem," Duncan said firmly. "The Great Oak is dying without it."

Rocky clutched the gem tighter. "But it's so beautiful! Why should I give it back?"

Duncan took a deep breath. "If you return it, I promise to show you something even more magical. Trust me."

———

Duncan dankte Benny und eilte los, um Rocky zu finden. Als er Rockys Bau erreichte, sah er den Waschbären, wie er das

Kernholz-Juwel bewunderte, dessen grünes Leuchten die Höhle erhellte.

„Rocky, du musst das Kernholz-Juwel zurückgeben," sagte Duncan fest. „Die Große Eiche stirbt ohne es."

Rocky umklammerte das Juwel fester. „Aber es ist so schön! Warum sollte ich es zurückgeben?"

Duncan holte tief Luft. „Wenn du es zurückgibst, verspreche ich dir, dir etwas noch Magischeres zu zeigen. Vertraue mir."

Rocky's curiosity got the better of him. "Alright, but this better be good."

Duncan led Rocky back to the Great Oak. As they approached, Duncan's coat began to shimmer and change colors, casting a mesmerizing light over the forest. The other animals watched in awe as Duncan's colors danced across the trees.

"Wow," Rocky whispered. "I've never seen anything like that."

With Rocky's help, they placed the Heartwood Gem back into the roots of the Great Oak. Almost instantly, the tree began to revive. Its leaves turned green again, and its trunk regained its vitality.

Rockys Neugierde siegte. „Na gut, aber das muss wirklich gut sein."

Duncan führte Rocky zurück zur Großen Eiche. Als sie sich näherten, begann Duncans Fell zu schimmern und die Farben zu wechseln und warf ein faszinierendes Licht über den Wald. Die anderen Tiere sahen staunend zu, wie Duncans Farben über die Bäume tanzten.

„Wow,“ flüsterte Rocky. „So etwas habe ich noch nie gesehen.“

Mit Rockys Hilfe legten sie das Kernholz-Juwel zurück in die Wurzeln der Großen Eiche. Fast sofort begann der Baum wieder zu leben. Seine Blätter wurden wieder grün und sein Stamm gewann seine Vitalität zurück.

The animals cheered and celebrated, surrounding Duncan and Rocky. They were hailed as heroes, and Duncan felt a sense of belonging he had never felt before.

"Thank you, Duncan," Squeaky said, his eyes shining with gratitude. "You've saved the Great Oak and our home."

Duncan smiled, his coat shimmering with the colors of joy and contentment. "I'm just glad I could help."

From that day on, Duncan was no longer just the donkey with the magical coat. He was a symbol of hope and courage, showing everyone that being different was a gift that could save the day.

Die Tiere jubelten und feierten, umringten Duncan und Rocky. Sie wurden als Helden gefeiert und Duncan fühlte ein Zugehörigkeitsgefühl, das er noch nie zuvor gespürt hatte.

„Danke, Duncan," sagte Squeaky, seine Augen leuchteten vor Dankbarkeit. „Du hast die Große Eiche und unser Zuhause gerettet."

Duncan lächelte, sein Fell schimmerte in den Farben der Freude und Zufriedenheit. „Ich bin einfach froh, dass ich helfen konnte."

Von diesem Tag an war Duncan nicht mehr nur der Esel mit dem magischen Fell. Er war ein Symbol der Hoffnung und des Mutes und zeigte allen, dass Anderssein ein Geschenk sein konnte, das den Tag rettet.

And so, Duncan the dazzling donkey lived happily ever after, his colorful coat bringing joy and wonder wherever he went. And in the heart of the forest, the Great Oak stood tall and proud, a reminder of the magic that could be found in the most unexpected places.

Und so lebte Duncan, der bezaubernde Esel, glücklich bis ans Ende seiner Tage, sein buntes Fell brachte überall Freude und Staunen. Und im Herzen des Waldes stand die Große Eiche hoch und stolz, eine Erinnerung an die Magie, die an den unerwartetsten Orten gefunden werden konnte.

Clara the Clever Cat - Clara, die kluge Katze

In the charming little town of Purrington, there lived a cat named Clara. But Clara was no ordinary cat. She had a knack for solving mysteries and helping her fellow townsfolk with her sharp mind and quick reflexes. Her fur was as sleek as midnight, and her eyes sparkled with a mischievous glint that suggested she always knew more than she let on.

In der reizenden kleinen Stadt Purrington lebte eine Katze namens Clara. Aber Clara war keine gewöhnliche Katze. Sie hatte ein Talent dafür, Rätsel zu lösen und ihren Mitbürgern mit ihrem scharfen Verstand und schnellen Reflexen zu helfen. Ihr Fell war so glatt wie Mitternacht und ihre Augen funkelten mit einem schelmischen Glanz, der andeutete, dass sie immer mehr wusste, als sie zugab.

Clara lived in a cozy attic apartment above the town's bakery, run by Mrs. Butterworth, a kind elderly woman who baked the best pastries in all of Purrington. Clara often helped Mrs. Butterworth by catching mice and delivering messages to the townsfolk. But what Clara loved most was solving puzzles and uncovering secrets.

One sunny morning, as Clara basked in the warmth of the bakery's kitchen, there was a frantic knock on the door. It was Timmy, the local paperboy, out of breath and wide-eyed.

"Clara, you have to come quickly! Something terrible has happened at the museum!"

Clara lebte in einer gemütlichen Dachgeschosswohnung über der Bäckerei der Stadt, die von Mrs. Butterworth geführt wurde, einer freundlichen älteren Dame, die die besten Gebäckstücke in ganz Purrington backte. Clara half Mrs. Butterworth oft, indem sie Mäuse fing und Nachrichten an die Stadtbewohner überbrachte. Aber was Clara am meisten liebte, war es, Rätsel zu lösen und Geheimnisse zu lüften.

Eines sonnigen Morgens, als Clara sich in der Wärme der Bäckereiküche sonnte, klopfte es hektisch an die Tür. Es war Timmy, der örtliche Zeitungsjunge, außer Atem und mit weit aufgerissenen Augen.

„Clara, du musst schnell kommen! Etwas Schreckliches ist im Museum passiert!"

Clara's ears perked up. "What's wrong, Timmy?"

Timmy took a deep breath. "The Golden Whisker statue has been stolen! The mayor is beside himself and the whole town is in a panic!"

Clara knew she had to act fast. She grabbed her trusty magnifying glass and followed Timmy to the Purrington Museum. When they arrived, the mayor, Mr. Whiskerton, was pacing back and forth in front of the museum, looking extremely worried.

"Oh, Clara! Thank goodness you're here," Mr. Whiskerton exclaimed. "The Golden Whisker is our town's most prized possession. If we don't find it soon, it could spell disaster for Purrington's annual festival!"

Claras Ohren stellten sich auf. „Was ist los, Timmy?"

Timmy holte tief Luft. „Die Goldene Schnurrhaar-Statue wurde gestohlen! Der Bürgermeister ist außer sich und die ganze Stadt ist in Panik!"

Clara wusste, dass sie schnell handeln musste. Sie griff nach ihrer zuverlässigen Lupe und folgte Timmy zum Purrington Museum. Als sie ankamen, lief der Bürgermeister, Herr Whiskerton, vor dem Museum auf und ab und sah äußerst besorgt aus.

„Oh, Clara! Zum Glück bist du hier," rief Herr Whiskerton aus. „Das Goldene Schnurrhaar ist unser wertvollster Besitz. Wenn wir es nicht bald finden, könnte das eine Katastrophe für Purringtons jährliches Fest bedeuten!"

Clara nodded, her mind already racing with possibilities. "Don't worry, Mr. Whiskerton. I'll find the Golden Whisker. Now, tell me everything you know about the theft."

Mr. Whiskerton explained that the Golden Whisker had been stolen during the night. The museum's security guard, a sleepy old hound named Rufus, had heard a noise but saw nothing unusual when he checked.

Clara inspected the scene carefully. She noticed a small tuft of fur caught on a display case. Examining it closely, she recognized it as raccoon fur. "Aha! Our thief is a raccoon," she said.

Clara nickte, ihr Verstand ratterte bereits mit Möglichkeiten. „Keine Sorge, Herr Whiskerton. Ich werde das Goldene Schnurrhaar finden. Erzählen Sie mir jetzt alles, was Sie über den Diebstahl wissen."

Herr Whiskerton erklärte, dass das Goldene Schnurrhaar während der Nacht gestohlen worden war. Der Sicherheitswachmann des Museums, ein verschlafener alter Hund namens Rufus, hatte ein Geräusch gehört, aber nichts Ungewöhnliches gesehen, als er nachsah.

Clara untersuchte die Szene sorgfältig. Sie bemerkte ein kleines Fellbüschel, das an einer Vitrine hängen geblieben war. Bei genauerer Betrachtung erkannte sie es als Waschbärfell. „Aha! Unser Dieb ist ein Waschbär," sagte sie.

With this clue in hand, Clara set off to find Rocky, the mischievous raccoon who lived near the edge of town. Rocky was known for his love of shiny objects and his sticky paws. Clara found Rocky lounging in a tree, nibbling on a stolen apple.

"Hello, Rocky," Clara called up. "I need to ask you about the Golden Whisker."

Rocky's eyes widened, and he nearly dropped his apple. "W-what about it?"

Clara narrowed her eyes. "I found some of your fur at the scene. Do you know anything about it?"

———————

Mit diesem Hinweis in der Hand machte sich Clara auf den Weg, um Rocky zu finden, den schelmischen Waschbären, der am Stadtrand lebte. Rocky war bekannt für seine Liebe zu glänzenden Objekten und seine klebrigen Pfoten. Clara fand Rocky, wie er in einem Baum faulenzte und an einem gestohlenen Apfel knabberte.

„Hallo, Rocky," rief Clara nach oben. „Ich muss dich nach dem Goldenen Schnurrhaar fragen."

Rockys Augen weiteten sich und er ließ fast seinen Apfel fallen. „W-was ist damit?"

Clara verengte die Augen. „Ich habe etwas von deinem Fell am Tatort gefunden. Weißt du etwas darüber?"

———————

Rocky gulped. "I... I might have seen something. But I didn't take it! Honest! I saw a shadowy figure sneaking into the museum late last night. It wasn't me, but I was too scared to follow them."

Clara believed Rocky. He might be a troublemaker, but he wasn't a liar. "Thank you, Rocky. Can you describe this figure?"

Rocky nodded. "It was tall and thin, and it moved very quietly. That's all I remember."

Clara pondered this new information. "A tall, thin figure who moves quietly... I need to check the garden behind the museum."

Rocky schluckte. „Ich... ich könnte etwas gesehen haben. Aber ich habe es nicht genommen! Ehrlich! Ich habe eine schattenhafte Gestalt gesehen, die spät in der Nacht ins Museum geschlichen ist. Ich war es nicht, aber ich hatte zu viel Angst, ihnen zu folgen."

Clara glaubte Rocky. Er mochte ein Unruhestifter sein, aber er war kein Lügner. „Danke, Rocky. Kannst du diese Gestalt beschreiben?"

Rocky nickte. „Es war groß und dünn und bewegte sich sehr leise. Das ist alles, woran ich mich erinnere."

Clara überlegte sich diese neuen Informationen. „Eine große, dünne Gestalt, die sich leise bewegt... Ich muss den Garten hinter dem Museum überprüfen."

Clara made her way to the museum's garden, where she found a trail of footprints leading to a hidden entrance. She followed the footprints and discovered a secret tunnel that led directly into the museum's storage room. Inside, she found a stash of stolen items, including the Golden Whisker!

Suddenly, a shadow loomed over Clara. She turned to see a tall, thin figure—Mr. Whiskerton!

"Mr. Whiskerton! Why?" Clara exclaimed.

Mr. Whiskerton sighed. "I didn't want to steal it, Clara. I just wanted to hide it temporarily to create a bit of excitement and draw more visitors to the museum. But it got out of hand."

Clara machte sich auf den Weg zum Garten des Museums, wo sie eine Spur von Fußabdrücken fand, die zu einem versteckten Eingang führten. Sie folgte den Fußabdrücken und entdeckte einen geheimen Tunnel, der direkt in den Lagerraum des Museums führte. Drinnen fand sie einen Vorrat an gestohlenen Gegenständen, darunter das Goldene Schnurrhaar!

Plötzlich erhob sich ein Schatten über Clara. Sie drehte sich um und sah eine große, dünne Gestalt – Herr Whiskerton!

„Herr Whiskerton! Warum?" rief Clara aus.

Herr Whiskerton seufzte. „Ich wollte es nicht wirklich stehlen, Clara. Ich wollte es nur vorübergehend verstecken, um etwas Aufregung zu schaffen und mehr Besucher ins Museum zu locken. Aber es geriet außer Kontrolle."

Clara shook her head. "You should have told the truth. Now, let's return

the Golden Whisker and make sure everything is put right."

Mr. Whiskerton nodded sheepishly and helped Clara carry the Golden Whisker back to its rightful place in the museum. As they entered the main hall, the townsfolk were waiting anxiously. Clara held up the Golden Whisker for everyone to see.

"The Golden Whisker has been found!" Clara announced. "And now we know what happened."

The crowd erupted into cheers and applause. Mr. Whiskerton stepped forward, looking contrite. "I'm very sorry for the trouble I've caused. I wanted to add a little excitement, but I should have known better. I promise to never pull such a stunt again."

The townsfolk forgave Mr. Whiskerton, understanding his intentions, and the Golden Whisker was placed back in its prominent display case. Clara felt a sense of accomplishment, not just for solving the mystery, but for helping everyone see the value of honesty and teamwork.

Clara schüttelte den Kopf. „Du hättest die Wahrheit sagen sollen. Jetzt lass uns das Goldene Schnurrhaar zurückbringen und sicherstellen, dass alles wieder in Ordnung ist."

Herr Whiskerton nickte schuldbewusst und half Clara, das Goldene Schnurrhaar zurück an seinen rechtmäßigen Platz im Museum zu tragen. Als sie die Haupthalle betraten, warteten die Stadtbewohner ungeduldig. Clara hielt das Goldene Schnurrhaar hoch, damit alle es sehen konnten.

„Das Goldene Schnurrhaar wurde gefunden!" kündigte Clara an. „Und jetzt wissen wir, was passiert ist."

Die Menge brach in Jubel und Applaus aus. Herr Whiskerton trat vor und sah reuevoll aus. „Es tut mir sehr leid für die Schwierigkeiten, die ich verursacht habe. Ich wollte nur ein wenig Aufregung schaffen, aber ich hätte es besser wissen sollen. Ich verspreche, so einen Stunt nie wieder zu machen."

Die Stadtbewohner vergaben Herrn Whiskerton und verstanden seine Absichten, und das Goldene Schnurrhaar wurde wieder in seinem prominenten Vitrinenplatz aufgestellt. Clara fühlte sich nicht nur für die Lösung des Rätsels, sondern auch für die Hilfe dabei, allen den Wert von Ehrlichkeit und Teamarbeit zu zeigen, stolz.

The next day, as Clara was relaxing in her cozy apartment, Mrs. Butterworth came by with a basket of freshly baked goodies. "Clara, I heard about your marvelous detective work! You're truly a hero."

Clara purred contentedly. "Thank you, Mrs. Butterworth. But I couldn't have done it without the help of the townsfolk and Rocky. Everyone played a part in solving the mystery."

Mrs. Butterworth smiled warmly and handed Clara a special treat—a pastry shaped like a golden whisker. "This is a token of our appreciation. For the cat who saved the day and brought a little more magic to Purrington."

Clara took a bite of the pastry and savored its sweet, buttery flavor. She looked out the window, where the sun was setting over Purrington, casting a golden glow over the town. Clara knew that there were many more mysteries to solve and adventures to be had, and she was ready for whatever came next.

Am nächsten Tag, als Clara sich in ihrem gemütlichen Apartment ausruhte, kam Mrs. Butterworth mit einem Korb frisch gebackener Köstlichkeiten vorbei. „Clara, ich habe von deiner großartigen Detektivarbeit gehört! Du bist wirklich eine Heldin."

Clara schnurrte zufrieden. „Danke, Mrs. Butterworth. Aber ich hätte es nicht ohne die Hilfe der Stadtbewohner und Rocky geschafft. Jeder hat seinen Teil zur Lösung des Rätsels beigetragen."

Mrs. Butterworth lächelte warm und überreichte Clara eine besondere Leckerei – ein Gebäck in Form eines goldenen Schnurrhaars. „Das ist ein Zeichen unserer Anerkennung. Für die Katze, die den Tag gerettet und Purrington ein wenig mehr Magie gebracht hat."

Clara nahm einen Bissen von dem Gebäck und genoss seinen süßen, butterartigen Geschmack. Sie blickte aus dem Fenster, wo die Sonne über Purrington unterging und das Städtchen in ein goldenes Licht tauchte. Clara wusste, dass noch viele weitere Rätsel zu lösen und Abenteuer zu erleben waren, und sie war bereit für alles, was als Nächstes kam.

<hr>

As the days passed, Clara continued her work as Purrington's beloved detective. She solved more mysteries, helped more friends, and always had a sparkle of curiosity in her eyes. The town's annual festival was a huge success, with everyone celebrating Clara's bravery and cleverness.

And every evening, as Clara looked out over the twinkling lights of Purrington, she felt a deep sense of contentment. She had found her place in the world, not because she was like everyone else, but because she was uniquely herself—a clever, courageous cat who made a difference.

<hr>

Mit den Tagen setzte Clara ihre Arbeit als geliebte Detektivin von Purrington fort. Sie löste weitere Rätsel, half mehr Freunden und hatte immer einen funkelnden Ausdruck der Neugier in ihren Augen. Das jährliche Stadtfest war ein großer Erfolg, bei dem alle Claras Mut und Klugheit feierten.

Und jeden Abend, wenn Clara über die funkelnden Lichter von Purrington blickte, verspürte sie ein tiefes Gefühl der Zufriedenheit. Sie hatte ihren Platz in der Welt gefunden, nicht weil sie wie alle anderen war, sondern weil sie einzigartig sie selbst war – eine kluge, mutige Katze, die einen Unterschied machte.

The Enchanted Storybook - Das Verzauberte Märchenbuch

In the bustling city of Storyville, where stories came to life in the blink of an eye, there was an old, dusty bookstore called "Whimsy's Wonders." It was run by a kindly old man named Mr. Whimsy, who had a twinkle in his eye and a passion for all things magical. Among the countless books on his shelves, there was one book that stood out. It was ancient, bound in deep purple velvet with gold leaf lettering that read "The Enchanted Storybook."

In der geschäftigen Stadt Geschichtenstadt, wo Geschichten im Handumdrehen lebendig wurden, gab es eine alte, staubige Buchhandlung namens "Whimsy's Wunder." Sie wurde von einem freundlichen alten Mann namens Mr. Whimsy geführt, der ein Funkeln in den Augen und eine Leidenschaft für alles Magische hatte. Unter den unzähligen Büchern auf seinen Regalen stach ein Buch besonders hervor. Es war uralt, in tiefem lila Samt gebunden und mit goldenen Buchstaben beschriftet, die "Das Verzauberte Märchenbuch" lauteten.

The Enchanted Storybook was rumored to be special, but no one knew just how magical it truly was. The book was said to have the power to transport readers into the very stories they read. But Mr. Whimsy kept it safely locked away, only taking it out for special occasions.

One rainy afternoon, a curious girl named Lily stumbled into the bookstore. Lily had a wild imagination and loved adventures more than anything. She was a regular visitor at Whimsy's Wonders, always excited to see what new stories awaited her. Today, however, she was in for a surprise.

Das Verzauberte Märchenbuch sollte etwas Besonderes sein, aber niemand wusste genau, wie magisch es wirklich war. Man sagte, das Buch hätte die Kraft, Leser in die Geschichten zu transportieren, die sie lasen. Aber Mr. Whimsy bewahrte es sicher verwahrt auf und holte es nur zu besonderen Anlässen heraus.

Eines regnerischen Nachmittags stolperte ein neugieriges Mädchen namens Lily in die Buchhandlung. Lily hatte eine wilde Phantasie und liebte Abenteuer mehr als alles andere. Sie war eine regelmäßige Besucherin bei Whimsy's Wunder und immer aufgeregt, zu sehen, welche neuen Geschichten auf sie warteten. Heute jedoch sollte sie eine Überraschung erleben.

Mr. Whimsy greeted Lily with a warm smile. "Hello, Lily! What a delight to see you. I have something very special today."

Lily's eyes sparkled. "What is it, Mr. Whimsy?"

With a mysterious grin, Mr. Whimsy led Lily to a corner of the bookstore where the Enchanted Storybook was kept. He unlocked the glass case and gently lifted the book out. "This is the Enchanted Storybook. It's been waiting for someone with a heart full of imagination and a love for adventure."

Lily's eyes widened. "Can I read it?"

Mr. Whimsy nodded. "But remember, Lily, this book is not like any other. Once you open it, you might find yourself in the middle of an adventure."

Lily's heart raced with excitement. "I'm ready!"

Mr. Whimsy begrüßte Lily mit einem warmen Lächeln. „Hallo, Lily! Es ist eine Freude, dich zu sehen. Ich habe heute etwas ganz Besonderes."

Lily's Augen funkelten. „Was ist es, Mr. Whimsy?"

Mit einem geheimnisvollen Grinsen führte Mr. Whimsy Lily zu einer Ecke der Buchhandlung, wo das Verzauberte Märchenbuch aufbewahrt wurde. Er schloss die Glasvitrine auf und hob das Buch vorsichtig heraus. „Das ist das Verzauberte Märchenbuch. Es hat auf jemanden mit einem Herzen voller Fantasie und einer Liebe für Abenteuer gewartet."

Lily's Augen weiteten sich. „Kann ich es lesen?"

Mr. Whimsy nickte. „Aber denk daran, Lily, dieses Buch ist nicht wie andere. Sobald du es öffnest, könntest du mitten in einem Abenteuer landen."

Lily's Herz klopfte vor Aufregung. „Ich bin bereit!"

Lily carefully opened the book, and as she turned the first page, a swirl of shimmering light enveloped her. The next moment, she found herself standing in a lush, enchanted forest with towering trees and sparkling streams. The air was filled with the sounds of magical creatures and the scent of blooming flowers.

She looked around in awe and spotted a talking squirrel wearing a tiny vest and holding a map. "Hello there! I'm Nutters. You must be Lily. The Enchanted Storybook has brought you here for a special quest!"

Lily was thrilled. "A quest? What do I need to do?"

Nutters waved the map enthusiastically. "You need to find the hidden Gem of the Forest. It's the only thing that can save this enchanted land from falling into darkness."

Lily's adventure had begun.

Lily öffnete das Buch vorsichtig, und als sie die erste Seite umblätterte, hüllte sie ein Wirbel aus schimmerndem Licht ein. Im nächsten Moment fand sie sich in einem üppigen, verzauberten Wald mit hohen Bäumen und glitzernden Bächen wieder. Die Luft war erfüllt von den Geräuschen magischer Kreaturen und dem Duft blühender Blumen.

Sie sah sich in Staunen um und entdeckte ein sprechendes Eichhörnchen, das eine kleine Weste trug und eine Karte hielt.

„Hallo! Ich bin Nutters. Du musst Lily sein. Das Verzauberte Märchenbuch hat dich hierhergebracht für eine besondere Quest!"

Lily war begeistert. „Eine Quest? Was muss ich tun?"

Nutters schwenkte die Karte begeistert. „Du musst das versteckte Juwel des Waldes finden. Es ist das einzige, was dieses verzauberte Land vor dem Eintauchen in Dunkelheit retten kann."

Lily's Abenteuer hatte begonnen.

As Lily and Nutters ventured deeper into the forest, they encountered various challenges. They crossed a rickety old bridge guarded by a grumpy troll who demanded a riddle to be solved before they could pass. Lily, with Nutters' encouragement, solved the riddle with ease and continued on their way.

They also faced a maze of thorns, where Lily had to use her wits to find a path through. Her determination and bravery led her through the maze, and they emerged into a beautiful glade with a sparkling pond in the center.

In the middle of the pond stood a pedestal with the Gem of the Forest glowing softly. But as they approached, a fierce dragon emerged from the trees, its scales glistening in the sunlight.

"Stop!" roared the dragon. "Who dares to take the Gem of the Forest?"

Als Lily und Nutters tiefer in den Wald vordrangen, stießen sie auf verschiedene Herausforderungen. Sie überquerten eine wackelige alte Brücke, die von einem mürrischen Troll bewacht wurde, der ein Rätsel verlangte, bevor sie passieren durften. Lily, mit Nutters' Ermutigung, löste das Rätsel mühelos und setzte ihren Weg fort.

Sie standen auch vor einem Dornengestrüpp, durch das Lily ihren Verstand nutzen musste, um einen Weg hindurch zu finden. Ihre Entschlossenheit und Tapferkeit führten sie durch das Labyrinth, und sie traten in eine wunderschöne Lichtung mit einem funkelnden Teich in der Mitte.

In der Mitte des Teiches stand ein Podest mit dem Juwel des Waldes, das sanft leuchtete. Doch als sie sich näherten, tauchte ein furchterregender Drache aus den Bäumen auf, dessen Schuppen im Sonnenlicht glänzten.

„Halt!" brüllte der Drache. „Wer wagt es, das Juwel des Waldes zu nehmen?"

Lily took a deep breath and stepped forward. "I'm Lily, and I've come to find the Gem of the Forest to save this land from darkness. Please, let us take it."

The dragon's eyes softened. "You are brave to come here and seek the gem. But you must prove your worth by showing kindness and courage."

Lily nodded. "I will do my best."

The dragon then challenged Lily to help him solve a problem. His wings were tangled in a net, and he needed help to free himself. Without hesitation, Lily and Nutters worked together to untangle the dragon's wings. The dragon, grateful for their help, allowed them to take the Gem of the Forest.

Lily atmete tief durch und trat vor. „Ich bin Lily und ich bin gekommen, um das Juwel des Waldes zu finden, um dieses Land vor der Dunkelheit zu retten. Bitte, lasst uns es nehmen."

Die Augen des Drachen wurden weicher. „Es ist mutig von dir, hierherzukommen und das Juwel zu suchen. Aber du musst deine Würdigkeit beweisen, indem du Freundlichkeit und Mut zeigst."

Lily nickte. „Ich werde mein Bestes tun."

Der Drache forderte Lily dann heraus, ihm bei einem Problem zu helfen. Seine Flügel waren in einem Netz verheddert, und er brauchte Hilfe, um sich zu befreien. Ohne zu zögern arbeiteten Lily und Nutters zusammen, um die Flügel des Drachen zu entwirren. Der Drache, dankbar für ihre Hilfe, erlaubte ihnen, das Juwel des Waldes mitzunehmen.

With the Gem of the Forest safely in hand, Lily and Nutters made their way back through the forest. The land began to brighten, with flowers blooming and creatures singing. They reached the heart of the forest, where Lily placed the gem on a pedestal. A burst of light filled the forest, and everything was restored to its magical glory.

Lily thanked Nutters for his help. "I couldn't have done it without you."

Nutters beamed. "And I couldn't have done it without you. You are truly brave and kind."

As the magical light surrounded Lily, she felt herself being gently lifted from the forest. When she opened her eyes, she was back in Mr. Whimsy's bookstore. The Enchanted Storybook was closed in her lap, and Mr. Whimsy smiled at her.

"Well done, Lily! You've completed your adventure."

***

Mit dem Juwel des Waldes sicher in der Hand machten sich Lily und Nutters auf den Rückweg durch den Wald. Das Land begann aufzuhellen, Blumen blühten und Kreaturen sangen. Sie erreichten das Herz des Waldes, wo Lily das Juwel auf ein Podest stellte. Ein Lichtstrahl erfüllte den Wald, und alles wurde in seiner magischen Pracht wiederhergestellt.

Lily dankte Nutters für seine Hilfe. „Ich hätte es ohne dich nicht geschafft."

Nutters strahlte. „Und ich hätte es ohne dich nicht geschafft. Du bist wirklich mutig und freundlich."

Als das magische Licht Lily umhüllte, fühlte sie sich sanft aus dem Wald herausgehoben. Als sie die Augen öffnete, war sie zurück in Mr. Whimsy's Buchhandlung. Das Verzauberte Märchenbuch lag geschlossen in ihrem Schoß, und Mr. Whimsy lächelte sie an.

„Gut gemacht, Lily! Du hast dein Abenteuer abgeschlossen.“

Lily looked at the Enchanted Storybook with awe. "Thank you, Mr. Whimsy. That was the most incredible adventure!"

Mr. Whimsy nodded, his eyes twinkling. "The book chose you for a reason, Lily. You have a special gift. Remember, the magic of the book is always within you."

Lily smiled and hugged the book close. "I'll never forget this adventure. And I'll always cherish the magic inside me."

With that, Lily left Whimsy's Wonders, her heart full of joy and her imagination brimming with new adventures. She knew that whenever she needed a spark of magic, all she had to do was look within herself.

Lily sah das Verzauberte Märchenbuch ehrfurchtsvoll an. „Danke, Mr. Whimsy. Das war das unglaublichste Abenteuer!“

Mr. Whimsy nickte, seine Augen funkelten. „Das Buch hat dich aus einem Grund ausgewählt, Lily. Du hast ein besonderes Talent. Denk daran, die Magie des Buches ist immer in dir.“

Lily lächelte und drückte das Buch an sich. „Ich werde dieses Abenteuer nie vergessen. Und ich werde die Magie in mir immer in Ehren halten.“

Damit verließ Lily Whimsy's Wunder, ihr Herz voller Freude und ihre Phantasie voll von neuen Abenteuern. Sie wusste, dass sie immer, wenn sie einen Funken Magie brauchte, nur in sich selbst schauen musste.

And so, in the little city of Storyville, where stories and magic intertwined, the legend of Lily and the Enchanted Storybook became a cherished tale. The book remained in Mr. Whimsy's bookstore, waiting for the next brave soul with a heart full of adventure to open its pages and embark on a new journey. And as for Lily, she continued to explore and dream, knowing that magic was never far away.

Und so wurde in der kleinen Stadt Geschichtenstadt, wo Geschichten und Magie sich miteinander verwebten, die Legende von Lily und dem Verzauberten Märchenbuch zu einer geschätzten Geschichte. Das Buch blieb in Mr. Whimsy's Buchhandlung, wartend auf die nächste mutige Seele mit einem Herzen voller Abenteuer, um seine Seiten zu öffnen und eine neue Reise anzutreten. Und Lily? Sie setzte ihre Erkundungen und Träume fort, in dem Wissen, dass Magie niemals weit entfernt war.

www.ingramcontent.com/pod-product-compliance
Lightning Source LLC
Chambersburg PA
CBHW061628130726
47996CB00003B/1177